PATH TO ENLIGHTMENT

A JOURNEY THROUGH INDIAN YOGA AND MEDITATION

DR. JAGADEESH PILLAI

Made with ♥ on the Notion Press Platform
www.notionpress.com

|| Dedicated to all wisdom seekers around the world ||

Contents

Prayer vii

About The Author ix

Preface xiii

1. The History And Philosophy Of Yoga: From Ancient Origins To Modern Practice 1

Part 1

2. The Science Of Breath: The Role Of Pranayama In Yoga And Meditation 7

Part 2

3. The Eight Limbs Of Yoga: A Comprehensive Guide To Ashtanga Yoga 13

Part 3

4. The Practice Of Asana: How To Align Your Body And Mind For Optimal Well-being 19

Part 4

5. The Power Of Mantra: Understanding And Using Sacred Sounds In Yoga And Meditation 23

Part 5

6. Meditation Techniques Of Ancient India: From Dharana To Dhyana 29

Part 6

7. Kundalini Yoga: Unlocking The Power Of The Serpent 35

Part 7

Contents

8. The Role Of Bhakti In Yoga: A Guide To Devotional Practices 41

Part 8

9. Yoga And Ayurveda: A Holistic Approach To Health And Wellness 47

Part 9

10. Yoga For Specific Needs: Adapting Yoga To Meet The Needs Of Different Populations 53

Part 10

11. The Yoga Of Consciousness: Advaita Vedanta And The Path To Self-realization 57

Other Books Of The Author 61

Contact 65

PRAYER

"Om Bhadram Karnebhih Shrunuyaama DevaahBhadram Pashyemaakshabhiryajatraah SthirairangaistushtuvaamsastanoobhihVyashema Devahitam YadaayuhSwasti Na Indro VridhashravaahSwasti Nah Pooshaa VishwavedaahSwasti Nastaarkshyo ArishtanemihSwasti No Brihaspatir DadhaatuOm Shantih, Shantih, Shantih"

The literal meaning of this mantra is: OM. O Gods! Let us hear auspicious words from our ears. O reverent Gods! Let us behold propitious visions from our eyes, let our organs and body be stable, healthy, and strong. Let us do that which is pleasing to the gods in the life span allotted to us. May Indra, inscribed in the scriptures, bring us fortune! May Pushan, the knower of the world, grant us prosperity! May Trakshya, who vanquishes enemies, bestow us with blessings! May Brihaspati bring us success!
OM Peace, Peace, Peace.

About The Author

Dr. Jagadeesh Pillai is a renowned Guinness World Record holder, writer, and researcher hailing from Varanasi, also known as the abode of Lord Shiva. With a Ph.D. in Vedic Science and a range of creative ideas and achievements, he is a true polymath. He is the author of more than 100 books including Research Publications. Although his roots can be traced back to Kerala, the people of Varanasi hold him in high regard and affectionately consider him one of their own.

Dr. Pillai has achieved four Guinness World Records in the following subjects:

"Script to Screen" - In this record, Dr. Pillai produced and directed an animation film within the shortest time possible, breaking the previous record set by Canadians. He has also received numerous national and international awards and recognitions for this achievement.

Longest Line of Postcards - For this record, Dr. Pillai created a line of 16,300 postcards on the occasion of the 163rd anniversary of Indian Postal Day. The event also included a questionnaire about the Indian flag.

Largest Poster Awareness Campaign - Dr. Pillai designed an awareness campaign on the subject of "Beti Bachao - Beti Padhao" (Save the Girl Child - Educate the Girl Child) to achieve this record.

Largest Envelope - In tribute to the Indian Prime Minister's

"Make in India" initiative, Dr. Pillai created a 4000 square meter envelope using waste paper to achieve this record.

Attempted - **70000 Candles on a 210 kg Cake** - To celebrate the 70th Indian Independence Day, Dr. Pillai attempted to light 70,000 candles on a 210 kg cake, which was recorded in World Records India.

Attempted - **Documentary on Dhamek Stupa of Sarnath in 17 Languages** - Dr. Pillai attempted to create a documentary on the Dhamek Stupa of Sarnath, dubbing it in 17 different languages. The result of this attempt is currently awaiting confirmation from the Guinness World Records.

Dr. Pillai is skilled in teaching the Bhagavad Gita, a Hindu scripture, and is popular among young people. He has helped many young people improve their lives through his motivational teachings.

In addition to teaching, he has composed and sung numerous Sanskrit Bhajans and patriotic songs.

He has also written and directed several short films and documentaries for awareness campaigns, and has volunteered with the police in both UP and Kerala to spread awareness about various issues through videos and photography.

Incredibly, he has produced and directed over 100 documentaries about the city of Varanasi, all on his own.

He has also helped and guided more than 25 boys and girls to achieve world records through creative and innovative methods. He is a multifaceted person who uses his intellect and the blessings given to him by God to excel in various areas. He is both a teacher and a student, always learning and teaching, and is able to master any subject he comes across.

He is a selfless social activist and motivational speaker who has overcome struggles and failures to become a successful and enthusiastic individual with a rich life experience.

In addition to his work with the Bhagavad Gita, he is also an efficient Tarot card reader, Astro-Vastu consultant, and a talented singer and composer. He has sung the entire Ram Charita Manas and Bhagavad Gita in his own compositions, and has sung the phrase "Lokah Samastha Sukhino Bhavantu" in 50 different languages. He is currently working on a detailed and scientific study of Vedas, Upanishads, Puranas, and the Bhagavad Gita. He has also composed and sung the Hanuman Chalisa and Gayatri Mantra in 108 and 1008 different compositions, respectively.

Awards - Four Times Guinness World Records, Winner of Mahatma Gandhi Vishwa Shanti Puraskar, Mahatma Gandhi Global Peace Ambassador, Kashi Ratna Award, Dr. APJ Abdul Kalam Motivational Person of the Year 2017, Mother Teresa Award, Indira Gandhi Priyadarshini Award, Bharat Vikas Ratna Award, Udyog Ratna Award, Vigyan Prasar Award, Poorvanchal Ratn Samman.

PREFACE

The journey towards enlightenment is a timeless and universal pursuit, and for thousands of years, the spiritual traditions of India have offered a wealth of wisdom and guidance for those seeking to understand the nature of the self and the ultimate reality. In this book, "The Path to Enlightenment: A Journey Through Indian Yoga and Meditation," we explore the rich history and philosophy of yoga and meditation, as well as the various techniques and practices that have been developed and refined over time.

Through the examination of ancient texts and the teachings of enlightened masters, we delve into the science of breath and the role of pranayama in yoga and meditation, the eight limbs of yoga and the practice of asana, the power of mantra, and the meditation techniques of ancient India. We also explore the more specialized practices of Kundalini Yoga, Bhakti Yoga, and Yoga for specific needs, and how they can be adapted to meet the needs of different populations.

In addition, we explore the connection between yoga and Ayurveda, the ancient Indian system of medicine, and how these practices can be integrated to offer a holistic approach to health and wellness. Finally, we delve into the philosophy of Advaita Vedanta and the path to self-realization.

This book is not just a collection of information but an invitation to embark on a journey of self-discovery and personal growth. We hope that it will serve as a guide and a source of inspiration for those seeking to deepen their understanding of the ancient wisdom of India and to discover the path to enlightenment.

I

The History and Philosophy of Yoga: From Ancient Origins to Modern Practice

The history and philosophy of yoga is a vast and complex subject that spans thousands of years and encompasses many different traditions and practices. At its core, yoga is a spiritual discipline that has its roots in ancient India, and its ultimate goal is to achieve spiritual enlightenment and union with the divine.

The earliest known references to yoga can be found in the ancient Indian texts known as the Vedas, which date back to around 1500 BCE. These texts describe a system of rituals and practices that were believed to bring the individual closer to the divine, and they form the foundation of the spiritual tradition that would later become known as yoga.

Over time, various sages and spiritual leaders began to develop and refine the practice of yoga, and different schools of thought emerged. One of the most influential of these early yoga sages was Patanjali, who is credited with codifying the practice of yoga in his text, the Yoga Sutras. This text, which was written around 200 CE, lays out the eight limbs of yoga, which include ethical principles, physical postures, breathing techniques, and the practice of meditation.

As yoga spread across India, it began to evolve and adapt to the different cultures and traditions it encountered. Over time, different branches of yoga emerged, each with its own unique approach and emphasis. Some of the most well-known branches of yoga include Hatha yoga, which focuses on physical postures and breath control, and Raja yoga, which emphasizes meditation and the attainment of spiritual enlightenment.

In more recent times, yoga has become a global phenomenon, with millions of people practicing it all over the world. Today, yoga is widely recognized for its many benefits, including improved physical health and flexibility, reduced stress and anxiety, and greater overall well-being.

Despite its many benefits, however, it is important to remember that yoga is first and foremost a spiritual discipline. At its core, yoga is about connecting with the divine and achieving a state of inner peace and enlightenment. Whether you are a beginner or a seasoned practitioner, it is essential to approach yoga with an open mind and a willingness to let go of your preconceptions and expectations.

The history and philosophy of yoga is a rich and fascinating subject that spans thousands of years and encompasses many different traditions and practices. From its ancient origins in India to its modern-day global popularity, yoga has always been about connecting with the divine and achieving a state of inner peace and enlightenment. Whether you are just starting out on your yoga journey or have been practicing for many years, it is important to remember that yoga is a spiritual discipline that requires an open mind and a willingness to let go of expectations.

"Yoga is the journey of the self, through the self, to the self."

- The Bhagavad Gita

ꕤ

II

The Science of Breath: The Role of Pranayama in Yoga and Meditation

The science of breath, or pranayama, is a fundamental aspect of yoga and meditation. The word "pranayama" is derived from the Sanskrit words "prana," meaning life force or vital energy, and "ayama," meaning control or regulation. Together, these words refer to the practice of controlling and regulating the breath in order to balance and harmonize the flow of prana, or vital energy, in the body.

Pranayama is said to have a number of benefits for both the body and the mind. Physiologically, it is believed to increase lung capacity, improve circulation and oxygenation of the blood, and reduce heart rate and blood pressure. Mentally, it is believed to reduce stress and anxiety, improve focus and concentration, and increase feelings of relaxation and calm.

There are many different techniques of pranayama, and each has its own unique set of benefits and applications. Some of the most commonly practiced techniques include:

Ujjayi: Also known as "ocean breath," this technique involves slightly constricting the back of the throat to create a soft, ocean-like sound when inhaling and exhaling. It is said to help balance the nervous system and reduce stress and anxiety.

Nadi Shodhana: Also known as "alternate nostril breathing," this technique involves alternating the breath between the right and left nostrils to balance the flow of energy in the body and reduce stress and anxiety.

Bhastrika: Also known as "bellows breath," this technique involves rapid, forceful inhales and exhales to stimulate the lungs and increase circulation. It is said to help boost energy and vitality.

Kapalabhati: Also known as "skull shining breath," this technique involves rapid, forceful exhales with passive inhales. It is said to help purify the lungs, improve digestion, and boost energy and vitality.

Pranayama is often incorporated into yoga practice, and it is also widely used as a standalone meditation technique. It is essential to practice pranayama under the guidance of a qualified teacher, as improper breathing techniques can cause harm.

The science of breath, or pranayama, is a fundamental aspect of yoga and meditation. It involves the practice of controlling and regulating the breath to balance and harmonize the flow of vital energy in the body. Pranayama is believed to have a number of benefits for both the body and the mind, and there are many different techniques of pranayama, each with its own unique set of benefits and applications. It is important to practice pranayama under the guidance of a qualified teacher.

"The ultimate goal of Yoga is to still the patterning of consciousness - to reach the source of thought and sensation and hear the silence of pure awareness behind the noise."

- Deepak Chopra

ຣ

III

The Eight Limbs of Yoga: A Comprehensive Guide to Ashtanga Yoga

The eight limbs of yoga, also known as Ashtanga Yoga, are a comprehensive guide to the practice of yoga. They were outlined by the ancient Indian sage Patanjali in his text, the Yoga Sutras, which is considered one of the foundational texts of yoga. The eight limbs of yoga are as follows:

Yama: ethical principles that guide one's behavior in relation to others, including non-violence, truthfulness, non-stealing, sexual restraint, and non-greed.

Niyama: personal observances that guide one's behavior in relation to oneself, including cleanliness, contentment, self-discipline, self-study, and devotion to God.

Asana: physical postures, which are designed to align and purify the body, improve flexibility, and increase physical strength and stamina.

Pranayama: breath control, which is designed to balance and harmonize the flow of prana, or vital energy, in the body.

Pratyahara: sense withdrawal, which is designed to help the mind focus and concentrate by withdrawing the senses from external distractions.

Dharana: concentration, which is designed to help the mind focus and concentrate on a single object, such as the breath or a mantra.

Dhyana: meditation, which is designed to help the mind achieve a state of deep concentration and inner stillness.

Samadhi: enlightenment, which is the ultimate goal of yoga and is described as a state of union with the divine.

Ashtanga Yoga is often considered a "path" or "method" of yoga because it is a step by step approach to achieve the ultimate goal of Samadhi. It is important to note that the eight limbs of yoga are not meant to be practiced in isolation but rather in conjunction with each other. Each limb supports the next, and the ultimate goal is to progress through each limb in order to achieve a state of enlightenment or union with the divine.

The eight limbs of yoga, also known as Ashtanga Yoga, is a comprehensive guide to the practice of yoga. They were outlined by the ancient Indian sage Patanjali and are designed to align and purify the body, improve flexibility, and increase physical strength and stamina, and ultimately achieve a state of union with the divine. The eight limbs of yoga include Yama, Niyama, Asana, Pranayama, Pratyahara, Dharana, Dhyana, and Samadhi. It is important to note that the eight limbs of yoga are not meant to be practiced in isolation but rather in conjunction with each other.

"Yoga is not a religion. It is a science, science of well-being, science of youthfulness, science of integrating body, mind and soul."

- Amit Ray

ꕤ

IV

The Practice of Asana: How to Align Your Body and Mind for Optimal Well-being

Asana refers to the physical practice of yoga postures. The word "asana" is derived from the Sanskrit word "as," meaning to sit, and "ana," meaning with comfort and ease. Together, these words refer to the practice of sitting in a comfortable and steady posture, which is believed to align and purify the body, improve flexibility, and increase physical strength and stamina.

Asanas are not just physical exercises, but also have mental and spiritual benefits. Practicing asanas helps to bring balance, strength, and flexibility to the body, which in turn, can help to bring balance, focus, and peace to the mind. Asanas can also help to release tension and stress from the body, and can help to increase concentration and focus.

When practicing asanas, it is important to focus on proper alignment and to listen to your body. This means moving slowly and mindfully into each posture, and not pushing beyond your limits. It is also important to breathe deeply and steadily during each posture.

It is important to start with basic postures and gradually progress to more advanced postures. It is also important to practice regularly and with consistency, as this will help to improve flexibility and strength over time.

It is also important to practice Asanas under the guidance of a qualified teacher, who can help you to learn proper alignment and technique and to modify postures as needed to suit your individual needs and abilities.

The practice of Asana refers to the physical practice of yoga postures, which is designed to align and purify the body, improve flexibility, and increase physical strength and stamina, and also help to bring balance, focus, and peace to the mind. It is important to focus on proper alignment and to listen to your body, move slowly and mindfully into each posture, breathe deeply and steadily during each posture, practice regularly and with consistency, and practice under the guidance of a qualified teacher.

"Yoga is the perfect opportunity to be curious about who you are."

- Jason Crandell

&

V

The Power of Mantra: Understanding and Using Sacred Sounds in Yoga and Meditation

A mantra is a sacred sound or word, often in Sanskrit, that is used as a tool for meditation and spiritual practice in yoga. The word "mantra" is derived from the Sanskrit words "man," meaning mind, and "tra," meaning to protect or liberate. Together, these words refer to the use of sound as a tool for protecting and liberating the mind from negative thoughts and patterns.

Mantras have been used for thousands of years in various spiritual traditions, and are believed to have powerful vibrational energy. Repeating a mantra during meditation is said to help to quiet the mind and to focus the mind on the present moment, which can lead to greater feelings of inner peace and calm.

One of the most well-known and widely used mantras is "Om," which is considered to be the sound of the universe, and is said to represent the ultimate reality or truth. Other common mantras include "Om Namah Shivaya," which is said to be a powerful mantra for self-purification and spiritual growth, and "Om Mani Padme Hum," which is said to be a powerful mantra for compassion and the attainment of enlightenment.

Mantras can be used in various ways, such as chanting, singing, or repeating silently to oneself. Some people choose to use a specific mantra for a specific period of time, while others choose to use different mantras for different purposes. It is important to find a mantra that resonates with you and that you feel comfortable repeating.

It is also important to note that the power of a mantra comes from its repetition and the intention behind it. The repetition of a mantra helps to create a connection between the mind and the sound, which can lead to a deeper understanding of the meaning of the mantra, and the intention behind it helps to focus the mind and the energy on a specific goal or outcome.

A mantra is a sacred sound or word, often in Sanskrit, that is used as a tool for meditation and spiritual practice in yoga. Mantras have been used for thousands of years and are believed to have powerful vibrational energy. Repeating a mantra during meditation is said to help to quiet the mind and to focus the mind on the present moment. The power of a mantra comes from its repetition and the intention behind it. It is important to find a mantra that resonates with you and that you feel comfortable repeating, and practice under the guidance of a qualified teacher if needed.

"Ayurveda is the science of life and the art of living. It is a holistic approach to health and wellness that seeks to balance the body, mind, and spirit."

- Dr. Vasant Lad

VI

Meditation Techniques of Ancient India: From Dharana to Dhyana

Meditation is an ancient practice that has its roots in India, and it is an integral part of yoga and many other spiritual traditions. The goal of meditation is to quiet the mind and to achieve a state of inner stillness, which is believed to lead to a deeper understanding of the self and the world. There are many different meditation techniques, and each has its own unique set of benefits and applications.

Dharana is one of the earliest known forms of meditation, and it is often referred to as "concentration." It is the sixth limb of the eight limbs of yoga outlined by Patanjali in his text, the Yoga Sutras. Dharana involves focusing the mind on a single object, such as the breath, a mantra, or an image. The goal is to achieve a state of single-pointed concentration, which is believed to lead to greater focus, clarity, and inner peace.

Dharana is often considered the first step towards the higher levels of meditation, such as Dhyana and Samadhi. Dhyana is the seventh limb of the eight limbs of yoga, and it is often referred to as "meditation." It involves achieving a state of deep concentration and inner stillness, in which the mind is free from thoughts and distractions. The goal of Dhyana is to achieve a state of "no-mind," in which the individual is able to observe the mind and the thoughts without becoming attached to them.

The ultimate goal of yoga and meditation is to achieve the state of Samadhi, the eighth limb of the eight limbs of yoga, which is often referred to as "enlightenment." Samadhi is a state of union with the divine, in which the individual is able to transcend the ego and to experience the ultimate reality or truth.

It is important to note that Dharana, Dhyana, and Samadhi are not separate practices but rather stages of a progressive journey. Dharana is the foundation for Dhyana, and Dhyana is the foundation for Samadhi. It is also important to remember that meditation is a process and it takes time, patience, and consistent practice to achieve the deeper levels of concentration and inner stillness.

Meditation techniques of ancient India have been

developed and refined over thousands of years. Dharana, Dhyana, and Samadhi are three of the most well-known and widely practiced meditation techniques in ancient India. Dharana is the practice of concentration, Dhyana is the practice of meditation, and Samadhi is the ultimate goal of yoga and meditation, which is a state of union with the divine. It is important to note that Dharana, Dhyana, and Samadhi are not separate practices but rather stages of a progressive journey, and it takes time, patience, and consistent practice to achieve the deeper levels of concentration and inner stillness. It is recommended to practice under the guidance of a qualified teacher if possible.

"Meditation is not a way of making your mind quiet. It's a way of entering into the quiet that's already there - buried under the 50,000 thoughts the average person thinks every day."

- Deepak Chopra

VII

Kundalini Yoga: Unlocking the Power of the Serpent

Kundalini Yoga is a form of yoga that focuses on awakening and harnessing the energy of the "kundalini," which is often described as a coiled serpent or energy located at the base of the spine. The word "kundalini" comes from the Sanskrit word "kundal," which means "coiled" or "circular." According to Kundalini Yoga, the kundalini energy is dormant in most individuals and can be awakened through specific yoga practices, including asanas (yoga postures), pranayama (breathing techniques), mantra (sacred sound), and meditation.

The purpose of Kundalini Yoga is to awaken the kundalini energy and guide it upward through the chakras (energy centers) located along the spine. When the kundalini energy reaches the crown chakra (at the top of the head), it is believed to bring about a state of spiritual enlightenment and union with the divine.

Kundalini Yoga is often considered a more advanced form of yoga, as it can be physically and mentally demanding and requires a strong foundation in the basics of yoga practice. It is important to practice Kundalini Yoga under the guidance of a qualified and experienced teacher, as improper practice can cause physical or psychological harm.

Kundalini Yoga practice includes a combination of physical postures, breath work, chanting, and meditation. The physical postures are designed to stimulate and balance the nervous system, and the breath work is designed to increase energy and vitality. The chanting and meditation help to balance the mind and emotions and to develop a deeper spiritual connection.

Kundalini Yoga is a form of yoga that focuses on awakening and harnessing the energy of the "kundalini" which is often described as a coiled serpent or energy located at the base of the spine. The goal of Kundalini Yoga is to awaken the kundalini energy and guide it upward through the chakras (energy centers) located along the spine, in order to bring about a state of spiritual enlightenment and union with the divine. Kundalini Yoga includes a combination of physical postures, breath work, chanting, and meditation, and it is important to practice under the guidance of a qualified and experienced teacher. Kundalini Yoga can be physically and mentally demanding and requires a strong foundation in the basics of yoga practice, it is also considered a more advanced form of yoga and it is important to be aware of the potential risks of improper practice.

"The path of Bhakti Yoga is the path of devotion and love for the divine, and the ultimate goal is to cultivate an unwavering devotion to the divine, which brings about a state of inner peace and spiritual enlightenment."

- Swami Sivananda

ꕤ

VIII

The Role of Bhakti in Yoga: A Guide to Devotional Practices

Bhakti is a Sanskrit word that translates to "devotion" or "love," and it is a central aspect of many spiritual traditions, including yoga. Bhakti yoga is the path of yoga that focuses on developing a deep, personal connection with a higher power through devotion, love, and devotion-based practices. The goal of Bhakti yoga is to cultivate an unwavering devotion to the divine, which is believed to bring about a state of inner peace, happiness, and spiritual enlightenment.

Bhakti yoga practices include singing devotional songs, reciting mantras, performing puja (worship) rituals, and reading sacred texts. These practices are designed to help practitioners develop a deeper connection with the divine, and to cultivate feelings of love, devotion, and surrender.

One of the central principles of Bhakti yoga is the concept of Ishvara-pranidhana, which means "surrender to the divine." This principle encourages practitioners to let go of their ego and to surrender their will to the divine, in order to achieve a state of inner peace and spiritual enlightenment.

Bhakti yoga also includes the practice of Bhakti-bhava, which is the cultivation of devotion and love for the divine in all aspects of life. This includes cultivating devotion in relationships, in work, and in daily activities, as well as in formal spiritual practices.

It is important to note that Bhakti yoga is open to people of all religions and spiritual backgrounds. It is a personal practice and one can choose to direct their devotion to a specific deity or to a more abstract concept of the divine. It is also important to note that Bhakti yoga is not limited to a specific set of beliefs or dogmas, it is a personal and spiritual journey that can be tailored to one's own beliefs and practices.

Bhakti is a central aspect of many spiritual traditions, including yoga. Bhakti yoga is the path of yoga that focuses on developing a deep, personal connection with a higher power through devotion, love, and devotion-based practices. The goal of Bhakti yoga is to cultivate an unwavering devotion to the divine, which is believed to bring about a state of inner peace, happiness, and spiritual enlightenment. Bhakti yoga practices include singing devotional songs, reciting mantras, performing puja (worship) rituals, and reading sacred texts. The practices are designed to help practitioners develop a deeper connection with the divine, and to cultivate feelings of love, devotion, and surrender. It is an open practice and one can choose to direct their devotion to a specific deity or to a more abstract concept of the divine. Bhakti yoga is a personal and spiritual journey that can be tailored to one's own beliefs and practices.

devotional [illegible] songs, reciting mantras, performing puj[illegible] [illegible] and [illegible] readings, [illegible]. The practices are [illegible] to help [illegible] cultivate a [illegible] deeper connection with [illegible] divine, and to cultivate [illegible] of love, devotion, and surrender. It is [illegible] open practice [illegible] one can choose [illegible] their devotion to a specific deity or [illegible] [illegible] of the divine [illegible] [illegible] spiritual journey that can [illegible] [illegible] rituals and practices.

"Kundalini Yoga is the science to unite the finite with Infinity, and it's the art to experience Infinity in the finite."

- Yogi Bhajan

ઇ

IX

Yoga and Ayurveda: A Holistic Approach to Health and Wellness

Yoga and Ayurveda are both ancient practices that originated in India and are closely related in their approach to health and wellness. Yoga is a spiritual and physical practice that focuses on the union of the mind, body, and spirit, while Ayurveda is a traditional system of medicine that focuses on maintaining balance and harmony within the body.

Ayurveda is based on the concept of three doshas or energies (Vata, Pitta, and Kapha) that are present in the body and govern its functioning. These doshas are said to be responsible for maintaining the balance of the body and mind. When the doshas are in balance, the body is healthy and in harmony. When they are out of balance, it leads to ill-health. Ayurveda uses a holistic approach to diagnosis and treatment, taking into account not only the physical symptoms but also the individual's lifestyle, diet, and emotional state.

Yoga, on the other hand, is a practice that aims to unite the mind, body, and spirit. It includes physical postures (asanas), breathing techniques (pranayama), and meditation. Yoga is believed to balance the body, mind, and spirit and to promote physical and mental well-being.

When combined, Yoga and Ayurveda offer a holistic approach to health and wellness. Yoga postures and breathing techniques are used to balance the doshas and maintain the balance of the body and mind. Ayurvedic principles are used to guide an individual's diet, lifestyle, and daily routine to maintain balance and harmony within the body. Together, these practices work to promote physical, mental and spiritual well-being.

Yoga and Ayurveda are two ancient Indian practices that share a holistic approach to health and wellness. Ayurveda focuses on maintaining balance and harmony within the body through diet, lifestyle, and emotional state. Yoga focuses on uniting the mind, body, and spirit through physical postures, breathing techniques and meditation. When combined, they offer a holistic approach to physical, mental and spiritual well-being. It is recommended to practice under the guidance of a qualified teacher if possible.

ℵ

"Advaita Vedanta teaches that the ultimate reality is the oneness of all things and that the individual self is ultimately identical to the ultimate reality."

- Swami Vivekananda

X

Yoga for Specific Needs: Adapting Yoga to Meet the Needs of Different Populations

Yoga is a practice that can be adapted to meet the needs of different populations, including those with specific needs or limitations.

For example, Yoga for seniors can be modified to include seated or chair-based postures, and can focus on building strength, balance, and flexibility. Yoga for children can be tailored to include fun, interactive, and age-appropriate activities that promote physical and emotional well-being.

Yoga for individuals with disabilities can be adapted to include modifications and assistive devices to make the practice accessible and safe for all. Yoga for individuals with chronic conditions such as arthritis, fibromyalgia, or heart disease, can focus on building strength, flexibility, and balance, while also addressing the specific needs of the individual.

Yoga for pregnant women can be modified to include postures that are safe for the mother and the baby, and can also help to prepare for labor and delivery. Yoga for individuals recovering from injury or surgery can be modified to include postures that are safe and appropriate for the individual's specific needs and limitations.

Yoga is a practice that can be adapted to meet the needs of different populations, including seniors, children, individuals with disabilities, those with chronic conditions, pregnant women and those recovering from injury or surgery. It is important to find a qualified teacher who is trained in adapting yoga for specific needs and to approach the practice with caution and safety in mind.

"Yoga is not just a physical practice, it is a journey towards self-discovery and the realization of the true nature of the self."

- B.K.S. Iyengar

ꕥ

XI

The Yoga of Consciousness: Advaita Vedanta and the Path to Self-Realization

The Yoga of Consciousness, also known as Advaita Vedanta, is a philosophical and spiritual tradition that has its roots in ancient India. Advaita Vedanta teaches that the ultimate reality is the oneness of all things and that the individual self is ultimately identical to the ultimate reality. This philosophy is based on the texts of the Upanishads and the teachings of the ancient Indian sage, Adi Shankara.

Advaita Vedanta teaches that the ultimate goal of human existence is to realize the oneness of the individual self with the ultimate reality, which is also referred to as Brahman or the Absolute. This realization is known as "Self-Realization" or "Enlightenment" and is believed to bring about a state of inner peace, happiness, and liberation from the cycle of birth and death.

The path to Self-Realization in Advaita Vedanta involves the cultivation of knowledge, discrimination, and devotion. Knowledge (jnana) refers to the understanding of the nature of reality, discrimination (viveka) refers to the ability to differentiate between the permanent and the transient, and devotion (bhakti) refers to the cultivation of love and devotion for the ultimate reality.

Advaita Vedanta emphasizes the importance of a qualified teacher or guru in the spiritual journey. A guru is considered to be a person who has already realized the ultimate reality and can guide the student on the path. The guru is seen as a source of guidance, inspiration, and support in the student's spiritual journey.

One of the key practices in Advaita Vedanta is self-inquiry or atma-vichara, which involves questioning the nature of the self and the ultimate reality. This practice is designed to help the individual transcend the ego and to realize the ultimate reality.

The Yoga of Consciousness, also known as Advaita Vedanta, is a philosophical and spiritual tradition that has its roots in ancient India. Advaita Vedanta teaches that the ultimate reality is the oneness of all things and that the individual self is ultimately identical to the ultimate reality. The ultimate goal of Advaita Vedanta is to achieve Self-

Realization, or the realization of the oneness of the individual self with the ultimate reality. The path to Self-Realization involves the cultivation of knowledge, discrimination, and devotion and the guidance of a qualified teacher or guru. Self-inquiry or atma-vichara is a key practice in Advaita Vedanta that helps the individual transcend the ego and realize the ultimate reality. Advaita Vedanta offers a holistic approach to spiritual growth, where knowledge, devotion and discrimination are integrated to achieve self-realization, inner peace and liberation from the cycle of birth and death.

Realization, or the realization of the oneness of the individual self with the ultimate reality. The path to Self-Realization involves the cultivation of knowledge, discrimination, and devotion and the guidance of a qualified teacher or guru. Self-inquiry or atma-vichara is a key practice in Advaita Vedanta that helps the individual discover the true self and realize the ultimate reality. [illegible] Vedanta offers a holistic approach to spiritual growth, where knowledge, devotion and discrimination are integrated to achieve self-realization, inner peace, and [illegible].

OTHER BOOKS OF THE AUTHOR

1. The Moments When I Met God
2. Kashiyile Theertha Pathangal
3. GURU GYAN VANI
4. Abhiprerak Gita
5. ASSI SE JAIN GHAT TAK
6. Hopelessness of Arjuna
7. The Soul and It's True Nature
8. Sense of Action (Karma)
9. Action through Wisdom
10. Action through Wisdom
11. THEORY AND PRACTICAL OF EVERY ACTION
12. LOGICAL UNDERSTANDING OF THE SUPREME
13. THE IMPERISHABLE SUPREME
14. Yatra Nishadraj se Hanuman Ghat Tak
15. Yatra Karnatak Ghat se Raja Ghat Tak
16. Yatra Pandey Ghat se Prayagraj Ghat Tak
17. Yatra Ranjendra Prasad Ghat se Dattatreya Ghat Tak
18. YaatraSindhiya Ghat se Gwaliar Ghat Tak
19. Yatra Mangala Gauri Ghat se Hanuman Gadhi Ghat Tak
20. Yatra Gaay Ghat Se Nishad Ghat Tak
21. MAA GANGA, GHATEN EVM UTSAV
22. Ganga Arti Dev Deepavali evam Any Utsav
23. Potentials of Digitalized India
24. VEDIC CONSCIOUSNESS
25. A Brief Introduction to Vedic Science
26. Kashi ke Barah Jyotirling
27. IMPACT OF MOTIVATION
28. Let's have a Milky Way Journey
29. Color Therapy in a Nutshell

30. Rigveda in a Nutshell
31. Yajurveda in a Nutshell
32. Samveda in a Nutshell
33. Atharva Veda in a Nutshell
34. Ayushman Bhava - Ayurveda
35. Srimad Bhagavad Gita and Upanishad Connection
36. Srimad Bhagavad Gita - an attempt to summarize each chapter.
37. Facts and Impact of Nakshatra
38. Astro Gems - NAVARATNA
39. Ekadashi - A Concise Overview
40. A Concise View of Hanuman Chalisa
41. Inspirational Gita
42. Nakshatraranyam
43. Summary of 18 Mahapuranas
44. Synopsis of 18 Upa Puranas
45. Rigvediya Upanishads
46. Shukla Yajurvediya Upanishads
47. Krishna Yajurvediya Upanishads
48. Samavediya Upanishads
49. Atharvavediya Upanishads
50. The Seven Great Sages
51. From Rocket Scientist to President Dr. APJ Abdul Kalam
52. The Visionary's Voice - Quotes of Dr. APJ Abdul Kalam
53. The Wisdom of Swami Vivekananda: Insights and Inspiration from a Legendary Spiritual Teacher
54. Ayurvedic Remedies from the Garden
55. Sages and Seers
56. Rising Strong – Motivational Stories of Women
57. Beyond Flames -Mystery stories of Funeral Ghat Manikarnika
58. The Origins of Tulsi: A Look at the Mythological Roots of the Plant"

59. The Holistic Cow: A Look at the Physical, Spiritual, and Cultural Importance of Cows in India
60. Arts of Healing
61. Exploring the Divine
62. Understanding Five Elements
63. The Etymology of Ram
64. Symbols of India
65. Voice of Change (About Speeches of Great Men)
66. She Speaks (About Speeches of Great Women)
67. Patriotism on Celluloid – Brief About Patriotic Films
68. The Music of Motivation: A Brief Guide to Inspirational Film Songs
69. Unlocking the Secrets of the Dashopanishads
70. A Cultural Mosaic
71. Ancient Traditions, Modern Minds
72. Ecos of Ancient Wisdom
73. Beneath the Surface
74. From Temples to Ashrams
75. Sages of the Subcontinent
76. The Art of Healling (Ayurveda, Yoga & Naturopathy)
77. Indian Kitchen
78. The Festivals of India
79. The Indian Epics Retold
80. The Power of Mantras
81. The Indian River Ganges
82. The Indian Architecture
83. Rites of Passage
84. The Indian Silk Road
85. The Indian Literature
86. The Indian Villages
87. The Indian Folks & Crafts
88. The Way of Buddha
89. The Ramayan of Tulsidas

90. Astrological Remedies
91. The Secret Power of Motivation
92. Secret of Developing your Inner Strength
93. The Secret Path to Motivation
94. The Art and Secret of Positive Thinking
95. The Secrets of Practicing Ethical Living
96. Indian Art and Painting
97. The Indian Herbalism
98. Bharatanatyam to Kathak
99. Exploring India's Astrological Remedies
100. The Indian Festival of Flowers
101. Indian Handicrafts
102. The Splashes of Joy – India's Colour Festival

CONTACT

DR. JAGADEESH PILLAI

PhD in Vedic Science

Four Times Guinness World Record Holder

Winner of Mahatma Gandhi Vishwa Shanti Puraskar and Global Peace Ambassador

Gemology, Astro & Vastu Consultant - Spiritual Counselor

Consultant for designing World Record Ideas

Efficient Tarot Card Reader

9839093003

myrichindia@gmail.com

drjagadeeshpillai@facebook

drjagadeeshpillai@instagram

jagadeeshpillai@youtube

www. JAGADEESHPILLAI.com

|| LOKAHA SAMASTHAHA SUKHINO BHAVANTU ||

9 798889 517580

Printed by Libri Plureos GmbH in Hamburg, Germany